AWAKENING
FAITH

A Guide for
Loving
Those Who
Leave the
Church

Kevin R. Scott

AWAKENING FAITH:
A GUIDE FOR LOVING THOSE WHO LEAVE THE CHURCH

© 2023 by Kevin R. Scott

ISBN (Print): 979-8-218-22737-1

ISBN (E-book): 979-8-223-26186-5

Cover design: Lauren Scott

To those with the courage to think for themselves
and embark on their own spiritual journey,
and to all those who love them.
May you experience unexpected growth,
greater spiritual awareness and maturity,
and all the love and support you need.

CONTENTS

START HERE

I have titled this part of the book as I have, because for many readers, the word *introduction* translates roughly as, "You can safely skip this material." But the next few pages contain crucial information for getting the most from this book. Even if you are typically an introduction-skipper, I strongly encourage you to start here.

My assumption is that you are reading this book because you are concerned about a loved one—a friend, child, spouse, significant other, or even a parent—and where their spiritual journey seems to be taking them. They're actively questioning, doubting, and criticizing people, institutions, and ideas you hold dear. They're espousing political views that seem contrary to faith. Maybe they're exploring other faiths—or no faith! You want to maintain a good relationship, but you also want your loved one to know how you feel. Above all, you want them to maintain a healthy relationship with Christ— but you suspect they're not really interested in your opinions.

When you try to address their changing beliefs, they shut you down.

You may wonder, *How can I have a healthy relationship with my loved one while remaining true to my faith?* That's where this book comes in. By reading and applying the guidance in this book, you will learn and internalize the best ways to think about and relate with your loved one for as long as they continue their spiritual journey. In the process, the book will invite you not only to remain true to your faith but to awaken your faith to an even higher level than you have previously experienced.

ACKNOWLEDGING YOUR PAIN

Let's take a moment, right here at the outset, to acknowledge together how painful it can be when a loved one embarks on a spiritual journey to places where you can't or won't follow. While one of my intentions for this book is to help you rise above those negative emotions to relate to your loved one in a meaningful, loving way, we must begin where we are. And I'm guessing that your loved one's recent attitudes about the Christian faith have you feeling some kind of way.

Your loved one's spiritual journey is likely to elicit several difficult emotions in you—surprise, confusion, sadness, fear, anger, disgust, and more. The feelings you experience during this time are personal and unique to you, and you are not wrong for feeling whatever you feel. The sooner you can identify, accept, and release those feelings—rather than trying to ignore, resist, or deny their existence—the better off you and your loved one will be.

FEELINGS INFLUENCE ACTIONS

It's never a good idea to ignore or deny what you're feeling. Instead, it's important to acknowledge your feelings and try to understand what they are telling you. In this case, your emotions are likely telling you that you believe your loved one is making a big mistake. Maybe they are; maybe they aren't—that's between them and the Creator. What's important for you right now is to recognize how you are feeling about your loved one and their spiritual journey. That's because your feelings influence your actions.

You've probably noticed this phenomenon before. When you get a good night's sleep, and your day starts off on a positive note, you're more likely to be friendly to the people around you and have conversations that feel encouraging and productive. Maybe you woke up in time to make coffee, have your quiet time, and even have a bite to eat before attacking the day's task list. A good start to the day can generate positive feelings that have a powerful impact throughout the day.

But some mornings, everything seems to go wrong. Your alarm doesn't go off, so you're not able to follow through on your normal morning routine. When you stumble out of bed, you stub your toe, and the physical pain causes you to react in frustration and anger. You're having negative feelings right out of the gate, and unless you put in the effort to turn your day around, those negative feelings can impact the way you interact with people throughout your day.

More than you realize, the way you feel about your loved one dictates how you interact with them. If you feel mostly negative, you will unintentionally have interactions with your loved one that will undermine your relationship with them. You might find yourself lashing out in anger and hurt, punishing them with silence, or even trying to manipulate them back into the fold so you can feel good about them again.

Such negative feelings, left unchecked, are bound to put uncomfortable distance between you and your loved one. They can make it impossible for you to be present in your loved one's life in any meaningful way. I've seen it happen more often than I'd like—and I'm confident it's not the result you want. But if you can find and focus on positive feelings instead, those interactions will go much better.

That's why I wrote this book—to help you rise above any negative feelings you're experiencing and to look at the situation from a divine perspective. That way you can have a positive relationship with your loved one even as they journey, and you can continue to have a significant role in their life.

FEELINGS FLOW FROM THOUGHTS AND BELIEFS

To manage and rise above our negative feelings, though, we need to understand where they come from. Our feelings flow directly from our thoughts. When we think good things are happening, we *feel* good. When we think bad things are happening, we feel bad. It's really as simple as that.

That's why emotions, when we take time to understand them, are extremely valuable. They help us understand where our mind is at. If we are feeling badly, we can trace those bad feelings back to where they originated in our thoughts. Likewise, if we are having a good day, we should be able to find the source of those happy feelings in our positive thoughts.

The key is cultivating awareness of the emotions that we're experiencing. When we are aware of our emotions, they can help us evaluate the way we are thinking.

For example, listen to what Paul said in his joyful letter to the Philippians:

> Rejoice in the Lord always. I will say it again: Rejoice! Let your gentleness be evident to all. The Lord is near. Do not be anxious about anything, but in every situation, by prayer and petition, with thanksgiving, present your requests to God. And the peace of God, which transcends all understanding, will guard your hearts and your minds in Christ Jesus. Finally, brothers and sisters, whatever is true, whatever is noble, whatever is right, whatever is pure, whatever is lovely, whatever is admirable—if anything is excellent or praiseworthy—think about such things. (Phil. 4:4–8)

Note that Paul told his readers how they should feel—joyful, non-anxious, grateful. How can Paul so confidently prescribe for his readers how they should feel? It's because he knew the secret to managing your feelings.

THE BIBLICAL WAY TO RISE ABOVE NEGATIVE THOUGHTS

It's not always easy, but it is always *possible* to change the way you feel about any situation.

First, let's talk about what *doesn't* work. You don't change your feelings by ignoring them. You also don't change them by sheer effort or willpower. You can't simply decide to be happy or joyful. It doesn't work. But what does work, according to the Bible, is to change the way you think.

Now, you might be thinking, *But I am absolutely sure my loved one is heading down the wrong path on their spiritual journey. How can I think positively about that?* The answer is found in verse 8 above. Instead of dwelling on the negative, focus on the positive—what is true, noble, right, pure, lovely, admirable, excellent, and praiseworthy about your loved one's spiritual journey.

Paul's advice here is brilliant, though it is rare to find people following it. In a nutshell, this book is about applying Philippians 4:8 to your relationship with your loved one—so that you focus on thinking about admirable, excellent, and praiseworthy aspects of their spiritual journey. It's OK, if you don't know how to apply this verse in this situation. This book will help you do it.

By focusing on the positive aspects of your loved one's spiritual journey, you will be able to maintain and even strengthen your relationship with them. You will continue to play a valued and significant role in their life. I know that's what you truly want, and embracing the positive is really the only way to make it happen.

MY QUALIFICATIONS IN THIS AREA

But who am I? I am a lifelong student of Christ. I started down the pathway to ministerial ordination at the age of 15.

I was trained to study the Bible in the original languages in Bible college and seminary. I was student body chaplain and graduated *summa cum laude*. I've served the church in various capacities throughout most of my adult life, which is now embarking on its sixth decade. My first book, *ReCreatable: How God Heals the Brokenness of Life*, was published in 2014.

Along the way, I've always sought to remain flexible and teachable—to laugh at myself if I ever thought I knew everything there was to know or had arrived at the pinnacle of maturity. As a result, my life has involved perpetual deconstruction and reconstruction of my personal belief system. My own faith and beliefs look much different now than they did when I was starting out. Rather than naïvely submitting to a system of doctrine with another person's fingerprints all over it, I now rely on my own research, experience, intuition, and connection with God to determine for myself what I do and don't believe. In other words, I've moved beyond indoctrination in another human's belief system (whether of Calvin, Arminius, Wesley, or whoever) to trusting the Holy Spirit's illumination of the truth in my own mind and heart.

In addition to participating in my own spiritual journey, I've raised three children to adulthood (and have high hopes for the fourth also reaching that milestone). All three of my adult children were raised in the evangelical church, and each has embarked on their own unique spiritual journey. For all three, I've been present with them throughout their deconstruction process and maintained a good relationship with each of them in their ongoing spiritual journeys (with high hopes for that to continue forever).

All that to say that I am intimately familiar with both the Bible and the evangelical church, as well as this process that so often leads people to question the Bible and part ways with the evangelical church.

WHAT ABOUT DECONSTRUCTION?

The spiritual journey your loved one is on is one that people both inside and outside the church often describe as *deconstruction*. But what is deconstruction? At its root:

> *Religious deconstruction means*
> *unthinking what is untrue,*
> *while seeking what is true.*

Some people say deconstruction is rooted in secular philosophy. While secular philosophy may have given it a name, people have been deconstructing their faith since ancient times. In fact, Jesus was a practitioner, as seen most easily in his words, "You have heard that it was said . . . , but I tell you . . ." (Matt. 5:21–22; 27–28; 31–32; 33–34; 38–39; 43–44).

Religious deconstruction is a search for truth, nothing more. I say this as a comfort to you. Jesus said, "Seek and you will find" (Matt. 7:7). Your loved one is seeking, and Jesus made a promise about that, which you can rest in.

Religious deconstruction often begins when a person sees a discrepancy between what they've been taught and what they see in the Bible. It also generally begins with the motive that is found in Jesus' words in John 8:31–32: "To [those] who had believed him, Jesus said, 'If you hold to my teaching, you are really my disciples. Then you will know the truth, and the truth will set you free.'" All of this is good news for your loved one—and you.

Unfortunately, truth-seekers like your loved one—people who have legitimate questions about how traditional Christian doctrine represents Jesus' teachings—rarely find a safe space within the church to explore answers to those questions and hear the Spirit speak truth to their hearts.

Pastors, church leaders, and church members all tend to be more comfortable around people with settled, traditional Christian beliefs. Questions like the ones your loved one is asking are only tolerated if they seem to reinforce the truth-seeker's belief in accepted doctrine. When it becomes apparent that the truth-seeker is thinking independently—not simply accepting the church's authority—they are often labelled as a troublemaker or some other negative epithet. It's no wonder, then, that so many truth-seekers with legitimate questions about the church's teachings end up leaving the church altogether. They are often made to feel that they no longer belong.

Stay with me now. I know this is tough to read. But I believe it can be different for you and your loved one. That's the reason for this book—so that your deconstructing loved one will know they still have a friend in you.

HOW TO USE THIS BOOK

This book is a tool to help you follow Paul's guidance to "think on these things" as your loved one seeks to follow Jesus' instruction to "know the truth." In it, you will find twelve *affirmations* or truth-statements. These are reliable, Bible-based statements that you can "think on" and incorporate into your way of thinking about your loved one's journey.

Each affirmation is a positive statement that counteracts a negative thought or feeling you may be experiencing about your loved one's spiritual journey. Each affirmation is followed by an explanation and some exercises to help you think it, feel it, and act on it. In that way, they can help you shape your thoughts, feelings, and behaviors to maintain a positive influence in your loved one's life.

The affirmations themselves are divided into three types: affirmations of faith, hope, and love.

The four **affirmations of faith** form a foundation on which you can build a positive response to your loved one's spiritual journey, based on your own beliefs about God.

The four **affirmations of hope** express realistic, positive expectations for your loved one's spiritual journey, based on the foundation of the four affirmations of faith.

Building on the affirmations of faith and hope, the four **affirmations of love** express your intentions for how you will be in relationship with your loved one.

Together, these twelve affirmations will guide you in continuing to have a meaningful relationship with your loved one, while still honoring and being true to your own beliefs.

WHAT IF IT DOESN'T WORK?

Before we dive in, let me address a question you might have about this book: Will it work?

The answer depends on what you mean by the question. If you're wondering whether reading this book and applying its principles will help you bring your loved one back to the evangelical church and a more traditional faith, I can't promise you that. But I can tell you that it's much more likely your loved one will end up in a good place spiritually, if you take this book to heart.

However, I also want you to know that there's a better question to ask—one that's more in line with the purpose of this book. That question is, Will this book help me grow stronger in my faith? And, if you take it to heart, the answer to that question is, yes, absolutely.

I know that your loved one's spiritual journey has been causing you pain, and I'm genuinely sorry for that. But I also want to say, as gently as I know how, that your pain is revealing an opportunity for you to grow in faith.

Faith doesn't only trust God when life lines up with your expectations. Faith is tested when life throws you a curveball. Now, this isn't the kind of test that God is grading you to see how you will do. It's the kind of test that pushes you to grow beyond your current level of strength.

Before your loved one embarked on their spiritual journey, it was easy for you to trust God with your loved one's spiritual life because they were already living it to your specifications. Now that your loved one is venturing out on their own, you have two choices. You can panic and try to exercise control over their life by guilt or manipulation. Or you can place your faith in the love, wisdom, mercy, and grace of God and trust that God is already doing more for your loved one's spiritual growth and wellness in this moment than you ever could.

The only life you are responsible for—the only one you can rightfully control—is your own. If you choose the first path, you will almost certainly drive your loved one away from you. That is not the result you want, but it's the result that many people get, because they don't know a better way. The purpose of this book is to show you a better way.

You might say, "But I don't have that kind of faith. I just see this ending badly for everyone."

I can show you how to have that kind of faith, and as a result, have the best chance of keeping your loved one in your life—all while maintaining your own spiritual integrity. It's all about awakening your faith to a higher level than you've experienced before.

The purpose of this book is not to change your loved one; it's to change *you*. It's to help you remain clear about your own thoughts, beliefs, and feelings, while also remaining connected to your loved one wherever their spiritual journey might lead. It's to awaken your faith to trust in God rather than your own designs.

Let's take our first step now into a larger, stronger faith.

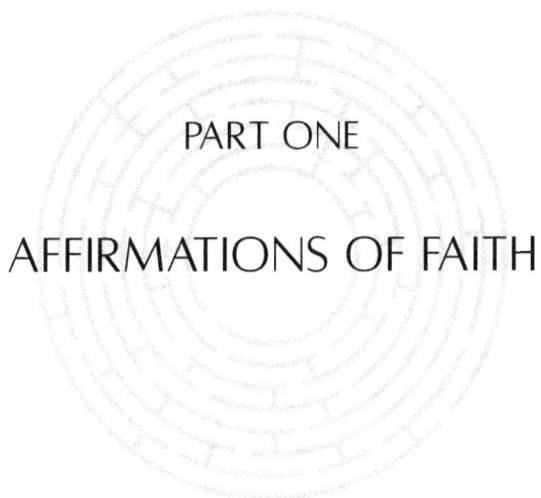

PART ONE

AFFIRMATIONS OF FAITH

AFFIRMATION 1

God's love for my loved one is infinite.

One of the first songs children learn at home or church is the familiar chorus:

Jesus loves me, this I know
For the Bible tells me so.
Little ones to him belong.
They are weak but he is strong.
Yes, Jesus loves me.
Yes, Jesus loves me.
Yes, Jesus loves me.
For the Bible tells me so.

We love "Jesus Loves Me" for its simple structure and straightforward message. It communicates foundational beliefs in a way that anyone can understand.

The core of this song's message is a powerful faith affirmation: "Jesus loves me." By singing the song, you assert your beliefs, strengthen your faith, and receive God's promises—all at the same time. When you sing it repeatedly, that simple affirmation can become a core belief that guides your life.

That's how affirmations work, and it's why we teach "Jesus Loves Me" to little children. The belief it creates has the potential to sink its roots deep, to the core of their being, and become a powerful foundation for the rest of their life.

USING AFFIRMATIONS

In this book, I will teach you twelve biblical affirmations that can guide your ongoing relationship with your loved one. Embracing these affirmations will transform the way you think, feel, and act. I promise you that, if you internalize these twelve affirmations, they will transform your outlook and guide you to having a life-giving relationship with your loved one, while remaining true to your faith and convictions.

Let's see how it works by working with Affirmation 1:

God's love for my loved one is infinite.

This is an affirmation of *faith*. It doesn't take more than a moment's thought for any Christian to know this affirmation is true, even if you haven't thought of it this way before.

The Bible affirms that God *is* love (1 John 4:8, 16) and loves the whole world without exception (John 3:16), including your loved one! God never *struggles* to love your loved one, because love is God's natural and constant state. This is tremendously encouraging, if you allow it to be. There has never been—and never will be—a moment when your loved one is beyond God's love. That would contradict what the Bible says about God's nature.

The Bible and Christian theology also affirm that God is *infinite*, meaning that God has no limits whatsoever. God is not limited by space or time. God is not limited by ignorance or weakness. And God is not limited by the free will of any other being, including your loved one.

It is theologically accurate, then, to say that God is "love without limits." That means it would be against God's character to withdraw love from your loved one—for any reason. This remains true, even if your loved one doesn't seem to return the love, since the Bible says that true love requires no reciprocation (Luke 6:32). God's love for us is not dependent on our love for God.

All this is good news for your loved one. So, I encourage you to put your loved one's name in the blank space below, and in full confidence, say it out loud right now:

God's love for _____ *is infinite.*

WATCH OUT FOR "YEAH BUTS"

If you're a thoughtful Christian, you probably grasp the truth of this affirmation, while simultaneously seeing one or more objections that seem to cast doubt on that truth.

I call such contradictory thoughts, *"yeah, buts." Yeah, buts* are those pesky, negative thoughts or beliefs that pop into your mind to distract you from thinking on good things (Phil. 4:8). They try to convince you that the situation is worse than you imagine or that the truth is not what it seems.

"Yeah, buts" are not from God; they come from our subconscious mind. They are negative beliefs that once seemed enlightening and helpful, so we embraced them—but they don't represent the whole truth. If we continue to entertain them, they inevitably drag our minds and hearts into negativity and doubt. They will cause us to see our loved one as something less than an ongoing recipient of infinite divine love.

MEDITATE ON GOD'S INFINITE LOVE

Perhaps no other truth so clearly meets every specification of Philippians 4:8 as infinite divine love. It is true, noble, right, pure, lovely, admirable, excellent, and praiseworthy. It is precisely the type of truth Paul urged us to keep at the forefront of our minds. Any thought that undermines our belief in infinite divine love should be banished from our minds.

In another place, Paul said that love is not only great but "the greatest" (1 Cor. 13:13). While theology has taught us that God's love is balanced or equaled by God's justice, Paul didn't even place justice in the top three. Of course not. God isn't justice. God is mercy. God is love. The reason Paul can confidently say that love is greater than faith and hope is that God is love—and nothing is greater than God or love.

Scripture teaches us to meditate on God's love. There is nothing negative, nothing destructive, that can come from meditating on infinite divine love. It is so pure and holy that we should meditate on it to the point that it becomes a core belief—one that is deeply engrained in our subconscious so that it becomes part of our internal operating system. Then, God's love will be the lens through which we see the world.

When you finally grasp the pure, holy truth of infinite divine love, it's best to just ignore the contradictory thoughts, the "yeah, buts." There's nothing good that comes from entertaining or dwelling on them. Much better to think on the reality of infinite divine love than to question and challenge it with contrarian thinking that seeks to limit the infinite.

However, I know that some of you have deeply engrained beliefs that you've learned from the church—beliefs you *think* you've learned from the Bible—that dare to challenge your belief in infinite divine love. To address such beliefs, it's sometimes best to deal with them head-on.

So, I'll address a couple of the more common ones.

GOD'S LOVE AND THE DOCTRINE OF ELECTION

First, I know that there's a whole brand of theology—a popular one—that imagines a God who loves some people and not others. Or that God loves some people in a special way that is withheld from other people. Same difference.

Believe me when I say that I'm not here to challenge anyone's core religious beliefs. That's not how I see my role in this book, and it's not something that I want to do or enjoy doing. But I will encourage you to focus on the positive affirmation of infinite divine love rather than the negating belief that some people aren't loved by God. Today, most humane theologians encourage the same, since they realize how devastating it is—to ourself and others—to treat another human being as unloved by God.

So, if that is your theological background and you hold that core belief, I encourage you treat everyone you meet as if they are elect. I invite you to join me in the assumption that your loved one is among the chosen ones. If you are instead driven by the fear that they may not be, you will almost certainly respond to them in ways that are unhelpful and even destructive. Avoid the temptation to suspect anyone, especially your loved one, is reprobate. Assume they are beneficiaries of infinite divine love just as much as you are.

GOD'S LOVE AND THE DOCTRINE OF HELL

A second possible objection I want to address briefly is about the doctrine of hell. Most Christians today have some type of working belief in eternal punishment for those who are not followers of Jesus.

Again, it is not my intent or role to challenge your core beliefs. What I will do is to encourage you, again, to focus much more on the positive affirmation of infinite divine love than on the doctrinal teaching regarding eternal punishment.

Fear—of hell or anything else—is never an effective driver of true spiritual transformation or growth. If you constantly think of your loved one as someone who is on the highway to hell, it will harm your relationship with them. Much better to consistently think of your loved one as someone who is the recipient of infinite divine love, beyond your wildest dreams or understanding.

So, in both cases, the best thing to do is ignore the "yeah, buts." They won't help you in any productive way. Instead, focus on the affirmation of the powerful truth:

God's love for _____ *is infinite.*

MAKING OUR AFFIRMATIONS STICK

Now, if we want these twelve affirmations to become core beliefs, we must do three things with them. First, we must think or meditate on them. Second, we must feel the truth of them. Third, we must begin to arrange our actions based on them. The more we think, feel, and act on these affirmations, the more quickly they will become a core part of who we are and will guide us in relating to our loved one.

So, along with each affirmation, I will give you a few thoughts about how to let the affirmation begin to flow through your thoughts, feelings, and actions.

PRACTICE AFFIRMATION 1

Here are some suggestions for practicing Affirmation 1.

THINK IT

1. Choose at least one way to express your belief in God's infinite love for your loved one—and then do it. You can write it, speak it, sing it, draw it—whatever is most meaningful to you. The important thing is finding a meaningful way to express it to yourself.

2. Consider posting reminders of God's infinite love around your home or workspace. For example, you might use a dry erase marker to write this affirmation on your bathroom mirror, so it's one of the first things you see—and think—each morning. The more often you bring the truth to mind, the more quickly it will become a part of who you are.

FEEL IT

1. Pay attention this week to the objections your mind raises to your affirmation of divine love for your loved one. Make a note of them, and then destroy each note as a way of taking each negative thought captive (2 Cor. 10:5). In doing so, you'll remove from your thoughts what's blocking you from feeling the truth.

2. One of the most practical ways to feel infinite divine love—for yourself and others—is through meditating on God's love. Spend fifteen minutes a day this week

meditating on God's love for yourself and your loved one. Find a quiet place where you won't be disturbed. Find a comfortable position, sitting or lying down. Then clear your head of every thought except one—infinite divine love. See in your mind's eye how much God loves your loved one.

ACT ON IT

Think of one way to show your loved one that you care about them this week—not in an "I'm concerned about you" way, but in an "I'm glad you're in my life" way. Then do it.

2

AFFIRMATION 2

God is with my loved on their journey.

In July 1979, advice columnist Ann Landers published a poem sent in by a reader, who told Ann that she had carried around a tattered copy of it for years. The authorship of that poem is the subject of a longstanding legal dispute, with at least three people claiming to have authored it. Most people know it as "Footprints in the Sand."

The poem, which is now widely available and deeply beloved, tells the story of a young woman, going through difficult times, who had a vision of two sets of footprints in the sand. She was greatly encouraged, since she interpreted this to mean that Jesus had been walking with her throughout her life, even at times when she was unaware of it. However, she was deeply disturbed to see that at one of the most difficult points in her life, the second set of footprints had disappeared. She wondered why God would abandon her at such a crucial point. Then the voice of God spoke and assured her that she was never alone, and that where she saw one set of footprints, God had carried her.

AFFIRMING GOD'S PRESENCE

This poem has comforted countless people over the years because it provides a tangible image of God being with us. While people may have many varying reactions to the thought of God's presence, for people of faith, it is a comfort.

The Bible clearly intends for us to see it this way. Consider God's word according to Isaiah the prophet:

> Do not fear, for I am with you; Do not be
> afraid, for I am your God. I will strengthen you,
> I will also help you, I will also uphold you with
> My righteous right hand. (Isa. 41:10 NASB).

This leads us to Affirmation 2:

God is with my loved one on their journey.

Like Affirmation 1, this is an affirmation of faith. Christian theology affirms God's omnipresence—that God is everywhere-present at every moment in time. In the Old Testament, David expressed this in a powerful way:

> Where can I go from your Spirit?
> Where can I flee from your presence?
> If I go up to the heavens, you are there;
> if I make my bed in the depths, you are there.
> If I rise on the wings of the dawn,
> if I settle on the far side of the sea,
> even there your hand will guide me,

your right hand will hold me fast.
If I say, "Surely the darkness will hide me
and the light become night around me,"
even the darkness will not be dark to you;
the night while shine like the day,
for darkness is as light to you.

(Ps. 139:7–12)

What was true for David is true for your loved one as well. There is nowhere their spiritual journey could take them that is beyond the divine presence. It is impossible for them to *leave God behind*. Wherever your loved one goes, God will be with them. This is true in the spiritual sense just as much as it is in the physical sense.

BUT IS GOD ON MY LOVED ONE'S "SIDE"?

Even as we consider the reality of God's presence in your loved one's journey, you may have already noticed some "yeah, buts" rising from your subconscious mind. Maybe you think, Sure, God is with them in the physical sense, but is God *with* with them? In other words, is God on their side?

It's a valid question. That's why we started with an affirmation of God's infinite love. If God's love for your loved one is infinite, there can be no question of whether God is on their side. Of course, God is with them in this way. God's love knows no end. God will never not love. There is nowhere your loved one can go and be outside of God's presence. And there is no way your loved one can slip beyond God's infinite love.

Your loved one's journey may take them into and through some places that seem particularly dark to you. You may feel that they are rejecting God. They may even *say* that they are rejecting God. When they enter such dark valleys, you may feel compelled to warn them to turn back on their journey. But turning back is rarely the right answer. The way is most often not *back*, but *through*. And most people emerge from the journey with more faith, not less.

No, you can't accompany them on their journey, but that's okay. Because you believe and have faith that God is always with them, even when you are not. Plus, you know that God always loves them with infinite love, a love that far exceeds your own great love for them.

WHAT IF THEY REJECT GOD?

You might think, *But what if my loved one rejects God?*

What if they do? What are you going to do about it? Sit there and worry yourself to death? Who will that help? There is nothing you can say or do to change the outcome of your loved one's spiritual journey. But one thing you can do—you can trust in an infinitely loving and merciful God to be present with your loved one as long as they live.

Truly, the best you can do is to lean in to and internalize the truth. Personalize it with your loved one's name and say it out loud:

God is with _____ on their journey.

It's an opportunity to awaken your faith to a new level. Keep in mind that we see a moment in time. We stress over current events. But God sees the whole journey from beginning to end. As often as we stress over our loved one's choices in the moment, we miss an opportunity to demonstrate faith in the infinitely loving and merciful God who is with our loved one every step of the journey.

So go ahead and say it again:

God is with _____ *on their journey.*

PRACTICE AFFIRMATION 2

Here are some suggestions for practicing Affirmation 2.

THINK IT

1. Read Psalm 139, and then close your eyes and take a few minutes to meditate on its truth in your loved one's life. What difference would it make if you truly believed God was not only with you but with everyone, everywhere, at all times?

2. Take some time to consider these questions: What beliefs do you have that make it difficult for you to believe that God is with your loved one, supporting them on their journey? Where do those beliefs come from? Do you need to change any beliefs to make room for this truth?

FEEL IT

1. Close your eyes and imagine your loved one in the presence of an infinitely loving and infinitely merciful God. Imagine what it would feel like to know that your loved one is perfectly safe and that there is no need for you to worry about them, since God is with them. Then speak the affirmation, in your mind or out loud, until you feel your concern subside:

God is with _____ on their journey.

2. The key to changing our feelings is to change our thinking. When you catch yourself thinking of your loved one as "far from God" or "drifting away from God," remind yourself that, wherever your loved one is, God is there too. Let that biblical truth become your default way of thinking.

ACT ON IT

Whether consciously or unconsciously, you may be tempted to distance yourself from your loved one, as a way of demonstrating your disapproval or treating them as "unholy." Resolve in your own mind and heart to feel close to your loved one no matter where their spiritual journey may take them. Continue to be involved in their life as you normally would, without needing to draw attention to their spiritual journey or set them apart in any way.

3

AFFIRMATION 3

God is at work in my loved one's life
in ways beyond my understanding.

As I look back over the 50-plus years of my life, there are many experiences and events that I understand much better now than I did when I was in the midst of them. Maybe you could say the same. For example, several years ago, I had a gut-wrenching experience that blindsided me, threw my life into chaos and confusion, and ultimately changed the trajectory of the rest of my life. People I considered friends seemed to turn on me. Statements I considered half-truths or blatant lies were told about me. Actions I considered unwarranted were taken against me. I felt lost and alone.

At the time, I couldn't understand what was happening to me, but in retrospect, I see how that experience was a necessary part of my spiritual journey and helped me to grow in ways that I never expected or even wanted to. That's not to say that what happened was justified or that I would choose to experience it all over again, but if it hadn't happened, I wouldn't be the person that I am today. And I'm grateful for the ways I've grown because of that experience.

OUR LIMITED PERSPECTIVE

We're almost always better at understanding and assigning value to our own spiritual journey in retrospect than we are in the moment. It shouldn't surprise us, then, if, looking from the outside, we are confused by what's going on in our loved one's spiritual journey. We don't have all the facts. We are limited in our ability to see the situation from our loved one's perspective, much less a divine perspective. Just this realization alone—that our loved one's spiritual journey will make more sense in retrospect—can awaken our faith.

That brings us to Affirmation 3:

God is at work in my loved one's life
in ways beyond my understanding.

This is our third affirmation of faith. Along with the first two—divine love and divine presence—it forms part of the faith foundation for your ongoing relationship with your loved one.

TRUST GOD'S INTENTION

This affirmation expresses a belief that God has a purpose for your loved one's life and acknowledges that God's ways are far beyond our own ways. Even if we don't understand in real time what God is doing in our loved one's life, God is still at work to bring our loved one along in their spiritual journey.

In his letter to the first-century Roman Christians, Paul said, "And we know that in all things God works for the good of those who love him, who have been called according to his purpose" (Rom. 8:28). This text offers a very clear promise that applies to your loved one: God has a good purpose for your loved one's life, and God is actively working out that purpose in this very moment.

It is not for us to understand everything God is doing in our loved one's life. We are not always capable of understanding our loved one's decisions or how God will use those decisions to bring about spiritual growth and maturity in our loved one's life. We are simply called to believe that it's true. And that means we can let go of the need to try to guide or influence our loved one's spiritual journey. God knows better than we do what our loved one needs to experience to attain the next level of spiritual growth. If we can't trust God with that, we can't trust God with anything!

But we *can* trust God with that. And that takes a lot of pressure off us. We are not responsible for what our loved one is thinking, feeling, or doing. And we can trust that God, who works in mysterious ways, is doing exactly what needs to be done for our loved one.

DOES THIS PROMISE REALLY APPLY TO MY LOVED ONE?

Some careful readers of the Bible's text will think they have discovered a loophole, whereby God is not obligated to work in their loved one's life to bring about good. They may point out that Paul specifically said, "God works for the good of *those who love him*" (Rom. 8:28; emphasis added). This, they think, proves that God *won't* work for the good of those who *don't* love him.

There are many things that could be said about this supposed loophole, but perhaps the most important thing is that it would be very strange behavior for an infinitely loving, infinitely merciful God to be looking for loopholes to get out of working for the good of your loved one. Is that really what we think God is like?

Paul didn't say that God *abandons* those who don't love him. He didn't say God treats them any differently at all. In fact, he went on to say that "God works for the good of . . . those who are called according to his purpose" (Rom. 8:28). If you believe your loved one has been given a purpose by God, then you have no reason to believe that God is looking for a loophole to get out of working for your loved one's good.

AVOID PREMATURE JUDGMENT

Not to mention, love is a complicated thing, and the words we say, the emotions we express, the actions we take don't always convey the truth of what's in our hearts. How many teenagers, in a moment of anger, have expressed hatred toward their parents—when the truth is that they love their parents deeply? So, even if your loved one seems to be expressing disdain for God right now, that doesn't necessarily reflect the true nature of their feelings. Likely, they are expressing frustration that is rooted in love.

So, be careful not to judge your loved one's life and love for God by a snapshot image of a moment in time or even a phase in life. Like angry teenagers who later discover as adults how wise their parents were, your loved one's anger at God is likely temporary and merely covering over deeper feelings of frustration or disappointment. None of this means that God has given up on them or abandoned them. In fact, it likely means that God is working overtime to guide them toward accomplishing their purpose in life.

One more thing: Note that Paul didn't say that God only works for the good of those who go to the right church, believe the right theology, or vote for the right candidates. Those are ways we define and sometimes divide ourselves, not God-given boundaries. God is infinitely loving and merciful and works for the good of *all* creation.

Say it aloud now, with feeling:

> *God is at work in _____'s life*
> *in ways beyond my understanding.*

PRACTICE AFFIRMATION 3

Here are some suggestions for practicing Affirmation 3.

THINK IT

1. Let Romans 8:28 be a key verse for you today or this week. Make an effort to memorize it and recite it to yourself at various points throughout the day. Or write it out and place it in various places at home and work, so you'll see it frequently. Each time you call the verse to mind, remind yourself that it applies equally to your loved one.

2. Consider the difference between faith and fear, in relation to this affirmation. What would it look and feel like to have faith that God is at work in your loved one's life in ways beyond your understanding? What does it look and feel like to be afraid that your loved one's journey will end in destruction? Why is it better to have faith than fear?

FEEL IT

1. Spend some time exploring why you feel the way you do about your loved one's spiritual journey. What makes it difficult to think that God is working all things for your loved one's good even now? Why might you assume that your loved one is going in the wrong spiritual direction rather than moving toward greater maturity?

2. Lean into the truth that "God works in mysterious ways." When you pray, express gratitude to God for the many ways God is working in your loved one's life to bring them spiritual growth and maturity. Avoid pleading with God to transform your loved one, but simply trust that God is already doing so. The more you act as if it's true, the truer it will feel to you.

ACT ON IT

Speak—to yourself and maybe even to your loved one—the words, "I am so excited to see where this spiritual journey will lead." Don't feel the need to justify your words by saying *why* you're confident it will lead in a good direction. Just express your excitement over where the journey will lead.

4

AFFIRMATION 4

God is pleased by my loved one's search for truth.

Christianity is built on faith, and yet I find that it's difficult for us to remember in a practical way the essence of faith. When we say we have faith, what it means is that we affirm something that can't be proven, and yet we believe it anyway (Heb. 11:1). If Christianity could be proven, then faith in Christ wouldn't be a virtue any greater than believing in gravity. Christianity wouldn't require faith to believe it; it would only require logic and good sense.

But Christianity, like all religions, is in a different category. It makes affirmations that aren't proven—can't be proven—beyond a shadow of a doubt. While there are certainly events and experiences that can be interpreted as supporting faith in Christianity, those events and experiences can always be interpreted differently and explained from a different framework of understanding. In a sense, believing in Christianity requires you to suspend your skepticism and just try it out to see if it works for you. This is not a criticism of Christianity in the least; it's simply acknowledging it for what it is—a system of faith and belief that, for many people, has given us a sense of meaning, significance, and purpose in life.

CHRISTIANITY AS A FAITH SYSTEM

Now, I know. It is much more than that. And many would say that Christianity is true in a way that outshines everything else we know. But it requires *faith* to see Christianity as truth:

- faith in an unseen God, who is unknowable except through divine revelation;
- faith that the Bible is actually the divinely inspired, infallible message of this unseen God;
- faith that we and our church are accurately interpreting the Bible in a way that gives us access to ultimate truth.

Please, please, please understand that I am not denying the truth revealed in Jesus Christ. I have always considered myself a follower of Christ, after all—and still do. So I'm not at all denying the deity of Christ or the message of hope that he brought to humanity. I'm simply reminding myself and those of you reading this book that the belief system we call Christianity is ultimately based on faith. Faith—not evidence or verifiable fact—is the only entry point.

Because of this, it should never surprise us when people—especially those who have been taught to believe in Christianity from a very young age—find themselves questioning their faith at junctures of their life. In fact, this is a healthy thing for us all to do. There is no virtue in blind faith.

We want to make sure we are always pursuing the truth—and not just what we've been taught to believe.

THE VIRTUE OF TRUTH SEEKING

That leads to Affirmation 4:

God is pleased by my loved one's search for truth.

This may be the most important affirmation in this entire book. The reason we tend to think negatively about people questioning or deconstructing their faith is that we assume they are rebelling against God, that they just want freedom from the moral constraints of religion. And because we assume that they are rebelling against God, we also assume that God is displeased with them, that they are on the verge of experiencing God's judgment or punishment.

But what if your loved one isn't rebelling against God so much as they are searching for the truth? That is the most gracious and sympathetic way for you to view your loved one's spiritual journey, and it is also likely the way they view their own journey too. After all, who wants to live a lie? Why would they intentionally turn from the truth to something they know is not true? The answer is, they wouldn't. And this can be a comfort to you. Your loved one is on a search for the truth. And you can be sure that, since they are seeking the truth, God is guiding them to it—even if the pathway doesn't look like you would prefer.

We might feel offended on God's behalf that they don't simply continue to accept on blind faith what they've been taught about God and the Bible and that they feel the need to explore the truth for themselves. But it's not actually God they're testing; it's what they've been taught about God by humans. I can assure you that God is not offended. People may be offended, but God is not. God is pleased when people seek to know the truth from fiction—and God helps them find it. As Jesus said, "You will know the truth, and the truth will set you free" (John 8:32).

So I want you to affirm it, out loud, with confidence:

God is pleased by _____'s search for truth.

That one realization—when it sinks deep—changes everything in your relationship with your loved one.

THE WAY TO TRUE SPIRITUAL MATURITY

There is a hard part to this realization, however. It's being okay with your loved one trusting their own ability to find the truth. You would likely prefer it if they simply trusted you and your testimony about the faith. You may be pleased if they trusted your pastor or your church instead of feeling the need to find their own way.

But can you see that the way to true spiritual maturity involves, not leapfrogging onto someone else's faith, but finding their own?

It's good to examine why you might prefer for your loved one the shortcut of vicarious faith, rather than the much longer, but more meaningful and life-transforming path of discovering the truth for yourself. For many Christians, they want to be assured of—or even control—the outcome. They want their loved one's journey to lead them on a circular path right back to where it started. And since they know they want their loved one to end up right where they started, they prefer for them not to make the journey in the first place. It seems so unnecessary.

But this precludes your loved one from learning important lessons on their way to true faith and spiritual maturity. Even more, it betrays a lack of faith in God to guide and support the journey in the best ways possible.

THE NATURE OF TRUE FAITH

You see, the ultimate faith is not being so sure of your own faith that you want everyone else's faith experiences to match your own. It's having faith in God to bring about divine purposes in your loved one's life—even when their journey looks very different from yours.

Are you ready to awaken to that level of faith in God? I think you are. You simply needed to see the situation for what it really is—and to recognize how it is inviting you to a deeper level of faith, right alongside your loved one.

WRAPPING UP THE FOUR AFFIRMATIONS OF FAITH

That brings us to the conclusion of this section of faith affirmations. Let's review.

1. God's love for my loved one is infinite.

2. God is with my loved one on their journey.

3. God is at work in my loved one's life in ways beyond my understanding.

4. God is pleased by my loved one's search for truth.

I encourage you to reflect and meditate on these four faith affirmations, letting them awaken your faith and sink deep into your soul. Continually acknowledge and reject the "yeah, buts" and other negative thoughts that enter your head. Focus instead on these positive affirmations that reflect a true faith in God.

In the next section, we'll transition to affirmations of hope about the outcome of your loved one's spiritual journey.

PRACTICE AFFIRMATION 4

Here are some suggestions for practicing Affirmation 4.

THINK IT

1. Try to identify in your own mind, without asking your loved one, what it is that your loved one currently believes. Do they believe in some form of God? Do they exercise some form of spirituality? Do they look to a specific set of writings for wisdom and guidance? Consider how each of these realities in your loved one's life points to an ongoing search for truth.

2. Meditate on John 8:32: "You will know the truth, and the truth will set you free." Think about how you believe God would respond to someone who is honestly seeking the truth. Consider how this might apply to your loved one.

FEEL IT

1. What level of faith does it require for you to believe that God is pleased with your loved one's search for truth? What "yeah, buts" interfere with your faith in this area? Determine to ignore the internal objections to think and feel that God is pleased with your loved one.

2. Imagine that your loved one is standing before God explaining their spiritual journey, and God is smiling over them, already knowing how the journey will end. How does God smiling on your loved one's search for truth

make you feel? What does this teach you about your own thoughts, beliefs, and feelings? Practice feeling just as pleased with your loved one's search for truth as you believe God is.

ACT ON IT

Every time you think about your loved one and their spiritual journey, determine to raise your level of faith. If the thought of your loved one makes you feel down, stretch your faith to believe that God is happy, and let it cause you to feel happy too. Continue raising your level of faith in this way, until it is no longer a question in your mind whether God is pleased with your loved one.

PART TWO

AFFIRMATIONS OF HOPE

5

AFFIRMATION 5

My loved one's heart is in the right place.

The affirmations in Part One were focused on faith—
what you believe about God and your loved one. The next
four affirmations are focused on hope—what you optimisti-
cally and realistically expect to happen in your loved one's life
because of their spiritual journey. If faith is primarily about
what we think and believe, then hope is mostly about what we
feel. These affirmations are designed to help you have feelings
about your loved one's journey that reflect faith rather than
fear.

AVOIDING KNEE-JERK REACTIONS

One of the most heartbreaking outcomes I've observed
when people embark on a spiritual journey like your loved
one's is that their pastor, friends in church, and loved ones respond in a knee-jerk way. It's almost as if they have two box-
es—one for people who are like us and one for people who are

not like us. As soon as someone begins questioning their faith or doubting the teaching they've received from the church, they are immediately taken out of the one box and placed in the other. I've personally had someone say to me, "I get the feeling you're not one of us anymore."

I know that, in most cases, people's responses come from a place of love. They genuinely want the person who is doubting their faith to "find their way back." But such knee-jerk responses cause damage and create distance. Despite best intentions, they do not communicate relational safety.

The rhetoric can be even more intense when the doubts and disagreements center on issues that touch both religion and politics. As I've observed this phenomenon in my own life and in the lives of others, I've been shocked to see how quickly a person can go from being a considered a "brother or sister in Christ" to being publicly called a "baby killer" or some other epithet—simply for having different views about the best ways to reduce the number of abortions that are performed in the United States.

RECOGNIZING THE RISK OF REJECTION

You may or may not be aware that when your loved one embarked on this spiritual journey that some call deconstruction, they were immediately risking several types of opposition, almost all of which likely came from people they consider friends and fellow Christians. Opposition like being:

- passed over for ministry opportunities;
- removed from teaching responsibilities, the worship team, or other prominent roles;

- considered an outsider or threat rather than an asset;
- labelled unfaithful, rebellious, a backslider, or even apostate;
- made a project by those who want to guide their journey or correct their beliefs;
- excluded from community, either subtly or more obviously;
- ostracized and rejected.

You may think I'm being overly dramatic, but I assure you I am not. When a person begins to question their faith and express thoughts or beliefs that are different from those accepted by the church, the rejection is real and near total.

Part of the reason for this book is to help you find your way to being one who is present in your loved one's life rather than being one who quietly ghosts them.

HAVING GENUINE HOPE

What will help you do that is to adjust your thinking about your loved one and their spiritual journey by having genuine hope and expecting good things to come from that journey. To be clear, I am not encouraging you to predetermine what a successful journey would look like for them. Instead, I want you to focus on the factors that point to positive results from their journey.

This leads to Affirmation 5, our first affirmation of hope:

My loved one's heart is in the right place.

Deep down, you know that it is.

REJECTING THE TYPICAL NARRATIVE

Often times, those in the church spin a narrative about people who are struggling with their faith—a narrative that is less than charitable and sympathetic. That narrative might include comments like these:

- They are following the trend.
- They want to be cool and popular.
- They want to be free to sin and live however they want.
- They are being influenced by the wrong people.
- They want to be accepted by the world.
- They're being deceived by liberal media.
- They were never really Christians.

Maybe you've heard some of these explanations about your loved one. Maybe you've thought or said some of them yourself. The thing about these statements is that every one of them is likely to be untrue about your loved one.

By far, most people who deconstruct their faith do so, not because of any outside influences, but because of what they've experienced in the church. That's why, instead of joining the common narrative, it's important that you trust your loved one's heart.

Before deconstruction, you likely would have described your loved one in positive ways: kind, loving, caring, faithful, warm, generous, or whatever other descriptions you may have chosen. Your loved one's search for truth likely hasn't changed even one of those positive qualities.

That's why it's so strange when other Christians suddenly turn on a person who is deconstructing and treat them as if they are under the sway of the evil one. A much more likely explanation is the one they would give to you if you asked—they want to believe the truth.

There's no reason to look "deeper" and see something malevolent going on beneath the surface. Such a perspective assumes that your loved one's spiritual journey is a bad thing—and remember, we've already chosen to believe that God is pleased with your loved one's search for truth. Instead, you can simply trust that the reasons your loved one gives are the real reasons.

BELIEVING YOUR LOVED ONE

Many church leaders reject the reasons people give for their deconstruction out of defensiveness and self-protection. Believing those who are deconstructing might mean that they would have to radically change the way they are doing church and ministry—a change they may not welcome.

But hopefully, you are in a position where you can choose to simply believe your loved one and trust that their heart is in the right place. If you don't have the freedom to do so, it would be good to examine why that is the case.

Your loved one needs to be believed and trusted. Otherwise, they will feel rejected and alone. One of the best ways you can support them is to believe—and let them know you believe—that they are accurately reflecting to you their experiences.

Affirm it with me now in an audible voice:

_____'s *heart is in the right place.*

PRACTICE AFFIRMATION 5

Here are some suggestions for practicing Affirmation 5.

THINK IT

1. This affirmation is about a feeling, but feelings are always based on thoughts. To change the way we feel, we need to change the way we think. In this case, your feelings about your loved one's trustworthiness will depend, in large part, on your previous relationship with them. Is your loved one, overall, a trustworthy person, or are they a known liar and deceiver? If they are generally trustworthy, you can be confident that what they are saying about the reasons for their deconstruction are true.

2. Keep in mind that you don't have to agree with everything your loved one thinks or believes—or follow them on their spiritual journey—to trust that they are being truthful and honest about their journey and that their heart is in the right place. Focus on your trust in your loved one, and it will solidify your relationship with them.

FEEL IT

1. Sometimes, trusting your loved one's experiences in their spiritual journey will call into question how much you can trust other people in your life, including your pastor and other church leaders. Instead of trying to resolve that question right now, remind yourself that, while you've always trusted your pastor and church

leaders, you've always trusted your loved one too. Live in that tension if you need to, until it becomes clear how to resolve the discrepancy.

2. You may be tempted to think your loved one has become "a different person." Short of mind-altering drugs, intense manipulation, or other extreme circumstances, that is unlikely to be the case. More likely is that you are now getting to know your loved one better than you have ever known them before. This is a good thing. Enjoy the feeling of seeing an authentic expression of who your loved one is.

ACT ON IT

1. If your loved one is open to it, ask them to share the reasons or experiences that led them to begin deconstructing their faith. Determine ahead of time that you will listen without judgment or defensiveness. Realize that they may express a high degree of frustration, and even anger, and be prepared to handle it calmly and without reacting in frustration or anger yourself.

2. In all your interactions with your loved one, assure your loved one that you believe them. Resist the temptation to reinterpret their story, give a different spin, or weave an alternate narrative. Simply trust your loved one by letting them share their story as they understand it. Any attempts to deny or diminish the impact of their narrative on their life are indicators that you still lack trust in your loved one.

AFFIRMATION 6

My loved one is smart enough to figure things out.

When I was in high school, I discovered a book by Josh McDowell called *Evidence that Demands a Verdict: Historical Evidences for the Christian Faith.* Looking back, this book was probably what sparked my love of Christian learning, especially in the areas of apologetics and theology. It fascinated me how this former skeptic constructed a compelling argument, based on historical evidence, that seemed to prove that Christianity was true. From there, it was a straight line for me to C.S. Lewis, Francis Schaeffer, N.T. Wright, Bible degrees, a Master's thesis, and ultimately ministerial ordination.

I loved learning about Jesus, the Bible, theology, and the Christian faith. I would read practically anything I could get my hands on about those topics. And through all my reading and learning, one thing became a clear conviction for me. If I honestly pursued the truth, I would find it. The world is a rational place. You do not need to take huge leaps of faith into

AWAKENING FAITH

the unknown to find meaning and purpose. They are there for you if only you seek it.

Part of my conviction was the importance of thinking for myself. If I merely accepted what I was taught, without exploring and examining the truth of the matter myself, I could not expect the truth to transform my life. But if I made it my life's purpose to seek the truth, the truth would find me. And as Jesus taught, the truth is what truly sets us free.

Part of what makes a loved one's deconstruction scary is the fear that they will be deceived and go down the wrong path to the "dark side." But nothing good can come from living in fear. Dwelling on your fear only serves to multiply it. Instead, it's much better to turn your fear over to God. You know you can trust God with it. You just have to let it go.

As Affirmation 6 says, you can trust your loved one too:

My loved one is smart enough to figure things out.

If someone said your loved one is intelligent and capable, you would readily agree. You might think, *I don't know where their head is at right now.* But that's just a way of saying that your loved one is currently thinking thoughts you aren't sure about. It's not a knock on their intelligence.

Sometimes you might hear someone who is deconstructing their faith described as "too smart for their own good." But that's just a way of saying, "I wish they would just trust."

It's important to know that, when people like your loved one question Christianity, there is usually a valid reason for it. They may have been victims of a toxic community, bad theology, or a traumatic situation. Or it could be something else.

70

It's not their *intellect* that's causing them to question their faith; it's their experiences. In fact, their intellect is what you can count on, in part, to guide them *through* their spiritual journey to the best outcome.

All of this is good news. Your loved one is an intelligent person who is seeking the truth. They are undoubtedly smart enough to figure it out sooner or later, whether you are there to witness it or not.

Now you may think, *Yeah, but it's not only about their intellect. It's about faith too.* And you are absolutely right. No matter how much authors, professors, and others may try to prove that Christianity is true and the only rational way to live your life, it ultimately comes down to a step of faith. Either you believe and embrace Christianity, or you don't.

Another question Christians don't often consider (but your loved one might) is, what version of Christianity do you believe? The reality is that there is not one but many ways to be Christian, and part of what your loved one may be considering is which "version" of Christianity makes most sense.

The point here, though, is that your loved one is smart enough to figure it out—to think for themselves, to examine all the evidence, to avoid being scammed by false religions and worldviews, and to do what makes the most sense to them. You might not understand the choices they are making right now. But you can believe and affirm that your loved one is smart enough to figure it all out in the end.

So, let's say it out loud again:

_____ *is smart enough to figure things out.*

PRACTICE AFFIRMATION 6

Here are some suggestions for practicing Affirmation 6.

THINK IT

1. Spend some more time mulling over the verse, "And you shall know the truth and the truth shall set you free" (John 8:32). Evangelical Christianity has an uneasy relationship with truth-seeking. On the one hand, it presents Christianity as an entirely rational religion that any reasonable person would choose. On the other, it gets nervous when people seek the truth outside certain narrowly drawn boundaries. Yet, all truth is God's truth, and truth-seeking is always the right thing to do, even if it requires rethinking aspects of your faith.

2. Too often, people reject what their loved ones learn on their spiritual journey because it doesn't fit with their preconceived notions of what true spirituality and Christianity are all about. Decide right now that you will keep an open mind about your loved one's spiritual journey and not reject what they're learning simply because it stretches you to think in new or different ways.

FEEL IT

1. You may be anxious about your loved one's spiritual journey because of subconscious beliefs about people who are "too smart for their own good" or who "don't have the faith to just accept the Bible." Take time to examine those beliefs. Often, they are rooted in an illogical belief that you personally have received the entire

truth about life and faith, and that anyone who thinks differently is wrong. To feel better about your loved one's journey, remind yourself that you are a finite individual who still has much to learn, as we all are.

2. Another reason you may be anxious about your loved one's spiritual journey is a subconscious belief that your church or faith tradition "has it right" and anyone who veers from what your church teaches is headed down the wrong path. To feel less anxious, remind yourself that there have been thousands of variations on the Christian faith over the years and that none of them has a corner on absolute truth.

ACT ON IT

Perhaps the best way to act on this affirmation is to choose not to act—not to send that meme or article you think will help your loved one see the light, not to suggest a book or movie you think will bolster their faith, not to try to influence their journey in any way. Simply trust that your loved one will figure it out.

7

AFFIRMATION 7

*My loved one is on the right path for them
(even if I can't see it right now).*

Take a few minutes to think back over your own life
experiences—

- the good times,
- the hard times,
- the true forks in the road,
- the times when you acted on impulse,
- the times when you carefully planned and plotted the
  future,
- the times when you "winged it,"
- the times when you were convinced you were making
  the right choice,
- the times when you had no idea what to do,
- the times when you were in a state of flow,
- the times when you felt stuck,
- the times when the world felt full of opportunities,

• the times when your options seemed severely limited.

Think back, in other words, over the entire trajectory of your life. Before continuing reading, take five to ten minutes right now to do that, using the bullets above as prompts for your thinking. Then pick up again here.

When you think back over your life, do you see your life progressing down a straight and narrow path that led to you becoming the person you are today? Or do you see a series of unexpected twists and turns that transformed your life in unexpected ways—some for the best, some not. If you're like most of us, you probably see a mixture of both—the intention of staying on a single path, along with the unexpected detours initiated by the curves life threw you along the way. Yet, all of the above brought you to where you are today.

Have you ever stopped to imagine what your journey might have looked like to other people—especially during the hard times? Sometimes we like to present an image of our lives—even to ourselves—as being all put together, from beginning to end. We sometimes like to pretend that our lives have progressed exactly as we have planned. For most of us, though, this just isn't reality.

AVOID PROJECTING UNREAL EXPECTATIONS

Today, as we observe our loved one's life, we may be tempted to place unrealistic expectations on what their journey should look like. We might prefer a journey that went straight for the destination, rather than the one that includes the unexpected twists and turns. However, placing such expectations on our loved one's life is unfair. And being anxious or frustrated when they veer off the path we had in mind for them—or even that they had for themselves—can be confusing and hurtful. We wouldn't have liked it if someone had done the same to us. (Or maybe they did; in which case, we ought to learn from that experience.)

We all wish we could save other people the trouble of learning through experience or growing through adversity; we especially want to protect them from going down what we see as the wrong path, even if that path might lead to valuable life experience they can't gain in any other way. You can't see where the path your loved one is on right now will lead and what results it will produce in their life. It feels like a dark, windy path to you, but keep in mind, that doesn't mean that it won't lead exactly where your loved one needs to go.

Since you're reading this book, there's a good chance that you have felt that your loved one is making a mistake. Remember that, from their perspective, they're choosing what seems like the best possible option. There may be more to the story than you know, and their options may seem more limited than you are aware. It's highly unlikely that your loved one decided on a whim that they just don't want to be a Christian anymore.

STRETCH YOUR HOPE MUSCLES

That brings us to Affirmation 7, which admittedly may require a stretch of your "hope muscles." But after all, Christians—of all people—ought to be characterized by faith, hope, and love. So here it is:

My loved one is on the right path for them (even if I can't see it right now).

I realize that this affirmation may at first feel like a shot in the dark and a hope without any foundation. But I hope that, upon further consideration, you will see that it follows logically from and builds on the foundation of the first six affirmations. To review:

1. God's love for my loved one is infinite.

2. God is with my loved one on their journey.

3. God is at work in my loved one's life in ways beyond my understanding.

4. God is pleased by my loved one's search for truth.

5. My loved one's heart is in the right place.

6. My loved one is smart enough to figure things out.

If all the above is true, and it is, then you have every right to hope that your loved one's path is leading them in the right direction.

God is intimately involved with your loved one's journey and knows where it's leading. Plus, as the events of your loved one's life unfold, they are making the best choices they know how to make in the moment. So, you can be reasonably confident that your loved one is on the path that will lead them to the right destination for them, even if none of it makes sense to you right now.

That is exactly what hope entails—trusting God and others for the outcome, when you don't understand what's happening and can't see what lies ahead.

EMBRACE HOPE

Too often, as Christians, we reject hope. We believe and expect the worst. It's ironic since the Bible teaches a much more positive outlook on life.

I am convinced that many of the negative things that happen in our lives, our nation, and our world happen because of our failure to exercise hope. For example, in a predominantly Christian nation, there is unquestionably a growing animosity toward Christianity. I believe, as a group, we have brought that animosity upon ourselves. First, we expected animosity. Then, we went and did things that created animosity toward Christianity for no good reason.

Here's an example on a personal level of what has happened on a national or even global level. Growing up in church, I was told numerous times and numerous ways that if I followed Christ, my non-Christian friends would reject me. What I learned from my experience is that if I treated people like reprobates, then yes, they would hate me. But if I treated them with love, joy, peace, patience, kindness, goodness, faithfulness, gentleness, and self-control (as the Bible prescribes in Galatians 5:22–23), then they welcomed me with open arms. On a larger scale, the lesson is that the growing animosity toward the Church today is not because the Church is growing more Christlike. Quite the opposite. We created the expectation of animosity, and then self-fulfilled the prophecy.

In much the same way, if you expect your loved one's journey to end badly, you are much more likely to say and do things to cause it to take a sharp turn away from you and the evangelical church. If, instead, you have hope and trust that your loved one is on the right path under God's nurturing guidance, then you will be experienced as more of a positive, helpful influence in your loved one's life.

So let yourself stretch, if need be, and exercise hope by affirming out loud:

_____ *is on the right path for them (even if I can't see it right now).*

PRACTICE AFFIRMATION 7

Here are some suggestions for practicing Affirmation 7.

THINK IT

1. In addition to hope, one other personal quality is required to make this affirmation your own belief. That quality is humility, as reflected in the second part of the affirmation. Ask God for the humility to recognize that you don't understand what's going on in your loved one's spiritual journey—and that's okay, because God does. Remind yourself that you don't need to understand in order to have hope that your loved one is on the right path.

2. Most of the objections one could raise to this affirmation make the mistake of thinking that there is only one path that will get your loved one to the destination God has for them. While Jesus said the path is narrow, he never said it was straight or that there is only one correct route. Be convinced in your mind and heart that there are many twists and turns one's life can take that seem "wrong" in the moment but still lead to greater spiritual maturity.

FEEL IT

Imagine a scenario in which your loved one continues on the path they are pursuing today, and when they reach the end of their life, they are embraced by God and told, "Well done!" Feel free to imagine whatever twists and turns in their journey you think would be necessary for them to receive that ultimate commendation, so long as they always continue forward in their journey rather than retreating. What does it feel like to imagine God affirming your loved one for choosing the path they are now on? Allow yourself to feel that feeling in real life, and as you do, affirm:

> *My loved one is on the right path for them*
> *(even if I can't see it right now).*

ACT ON IT

What would you do if you truly believed this affirmation were true? How would you act today and in the future? What kinds of things would you say and do with your loved one? What kinds of things would you avoid saying or doing? Sometimes, the best you can do is "fake it until you make it," to act your way into a new belief. So, determine today that, if nothing else, you're going to live as if you believe your loved one is on the right path.

8

AFFIRMATION 8

*My loved one's journey is
leading to greater spiritual maturity.*

It is disconcerting to watch a loved one enter an experience that you believe has the potential to harm their life. This is especially true when you feel that the experience is entirely avoidable—such as may seem to be the case with your loved one's current spiritual exploration.

If you have ever had small children in your life, you know the feeling of being responsible to protect them from harm. Perhaps you also know that parents and caregivers can go overboard in their desire to keep them from pain and sadness. Part of life is having experiences that help you learn and grow—and many of those experiences involve some level of hurt. If you were determined to never let a child experience any level of pain or frustration, they would never learn to walk or run or do so many of the things that bring joy to their lives and ours.

Most of us understand, at some level, that we have to give children freedom, within reason, to explore and experience the world around them, even if it means they may experience bumps, scrapes, and bruises. We know that's part of growing up, and we don't stress over it too much. As children grow into teenagers however, it can be hard to apply that same wisdom to the next stage of their life. Many parents have wrestled over where to draw the lines between giving their teenagers freedom to explore and experience life and keeping their teenager free from harm, safely in the fold.

Perhaps the most difficult parenthood transition of all, however, is acknowledging in your own heart that your child has become a full-grown adult and now has the responsibility to manage their own life, without the guard rails and limitations you have carefully managed throughout their life. There comes a time when you have to completely let go and allow your adult child to live their own life. This is much easier to do if you've been allowing your child increasing freedom and personal autonomy through their life, but even at that, there's usually some level of fear and anxiety that comes with acknowledging your child is now an adult and "on their own."

AWAKENING FAITH LEADS TO HOPE

Such moments call for faith—in God and in your child—and remembering how God uses all the experiences of our life, whether they seem positive or negative at the time, to bring us to maturity as human beings.

This brings us to our eighth affirmation—and the last one under the category of hope:

My loved one's journey is leading to greater spiritual maturity.

As with affirmation seven, it's helpful to remember that this affirmation is not wishful thinking, staying aloft on a wispy cloud. It is built on the solid foundation of the four affirmations of faith, and it works together with the previous three affirmations of hope.

THE FOUNDATION OF YOUR HOPE

You can be sure that your loved one's journey will lead to spiritual maturity because of what you believe about God. You know that God's love for your loved one is greater than you can imagine, that God is always with your loved one on their spiritual journey, that God is always working to accomplish your loved one's purpose in life even when you don't understand what's going on, that God is always happy when your loved one is searching for the truth—and that God will ensure they find it.

You can also be sure that your loved one's journey will lead to spiritual maturity because of what you believe about your loved one. You know, deep down, that your loved one's heart is in the right place. They have not suddenly turned into an evil person; they are simply looking to make sense of the life they have experienced. They are smart enough to discern the truth from a lie, and they know best what they need to explore and experience to arrive at a place of confidence in the truth. Their explorations may not be the same as yours, but they are ultimately leading to a place of greater spiritual understanding and maturity.

SPIRITUAL GROWTH RESULTS FROM SPIRITUAL EXPLORATION

Keep in mind that spiritual maturity is not about blindly believing what others have taught you. That's the way of spiritual dependence—and vulnerability to spiritual deception. If your loved one were to simply accept what they were taught based on the authority of a parent, pastor, church, denomination, or other spiritual authority, they would remain forever a spiritual child. Spiritual maturity involves coming to grips with spiritual truth for yourself.

Faith does not bypass a person's intelligence or their need to work out for themselves what they believe. Spiritual maturity requires personal faith—not a faith that is merely borrowed from some spiritual authority. Growing spiritually involves fully engaging your mind, heart, and will to choose who and what to place your faith in. No one can decide this for you—or your loved one.

That's why your loved one's spiritual exploration is actually a sign of spiritual growth, even if it feels uncomfortable or dangerous to you. Your loved one must choose for themselves where and how to invest their faith. So the journey they are on right now is essential to their spiritual growth.

HOPE IS YOUR BEST OPTION

Here's the truth: you won't know the outcome of your loved one's journey for quite some time—maybe even in your lifetime. Neither can you control it or make your loved one's decisions for them. The absolute best thing you can do is to be comforted by your faith in God and your loved one and to exercise hope, at all times, that your loved one's spiritual journey is the exact course they need to follow to get where God is leading them.

So, resist any urge to influence, manipulate, judge, or otherwise seek to force your loved one to take the path you prefer; instead, remind yourself that they need to choose their own path, and that God is walking with them, guiding them, and giving them the highest level of personal attention to ensure they arrive at the precise destination God has for them. This is what it means to place your hope in God rather than yourself.

Say it with me:

_____'s journey is
leading to greater spiritual maturity.

WRAPPING UP THE FOUR AFFIRMATIONS OF HOPE

That brings us to the end of the four Hope affirmations:

5. My loved one's heart is in the right place.

6. My loved one is smart enough to figure things out.

7. My loved one is on the right path for them (even if I can't see it right now).

8. My loved one's journey is leading to greater spiritual maturity.

As with the Faith affirmations, I encourage you to meditate on these four affirmations. Speak them aloud. Call them to mind often. And let them sink deep into your soul. The more they become a part of who you are, the more they will guide your relationship with your loved one in a positive direction.

PRACTICE AFFIRMATION 8

Here are some suggestions for practicing Affirmation 8.

THINK IT

1. If you are like most Christians, you will have to train your mind to believe that your loved one is actually on the path that will lead to spiritual maturity. This involves changing your internal programming that's causing you to think otherwise. Think of at least five ways you can reinforce this affirmation (My loved one's journey is leading to spiritual maturity) in your mind this week. Perhaps you can write it on a sticky note and place it on your mirror, make it your lock screen photo, or put it on your desktop background.

2. To make this affirmation as personal and meaningful to you as possible, find ways to restate it in your own words. Remember to keep your words entirely positive, without any hint of condition or negativity. Find at least five different ways to restate this affirmation in your own words.

FEEL IT

1. *After reading this suggestion, close your eyes and imagine what it describes.* Imagine your loved one in your mind's eye. Think about how much you admire them and the courage they are demonstrating in their desire to seek the truth and grow spiritually. Imagine yourself encouraging them, supporting them with your own faith, and releasing them to discover the truth in the way God

presents it to them. Then, express gratitude in your heart for the growth they are already experiencing, even if you can't personally see it.

2. Write down any objections you may feel to the idea that your loved one's spiritual journey is leading to spiritual maturity. After you've written them down, label them in bold letters: "Negative, Unhelpful Thoughts That I Now Reject." Then, destroy the list. If you wrote it on your computer, move it to the trash bin and empty the trash. If you wrote it on a piece of paper, crumble it up and throw it away or even burn it. As you destroy it, let go of those objections in favor of focusing on the hope you have built on the foundation of faith.

ACT ON IT

1. Determine to avoid thinking or saying anything negative about your loved one's spiritual journey—to yourself, to others, or to your loved one. Do so, based on the fact that you now believe your loved one's journey is leading them to discover the truth for themselves and that the outcome will be greater spiritual maturity for them.

2. The next time you have an opportunity to communicate with your loved one, tell them how proud you are of them. Tell them you are proud of how they are growing and where their life is heading. Be careful not to qualify your statements or indicate in any way that you know better where they are heading than they do (you don't). Simply express your trust in God and your loved one in words of affirmation to them.

PART THREE

AFFIRMATIONS OF LOVE

9

AFFIRMATION 9

*I support my loved one's desire
to decide what they truly believe.*

With this chapter, we move into the third category of affirmations. The first four were affirmations of Faith. The middle four were affirmations of Hope. And these last four are affirmations of Love.

Like the apostle Paul, I believe that love is even more important than faith and hope (1 Cor. 13:13). The four Faith affirmations and four Hope affirmations are important only inasmuch as they form a foundation that enables you to act in love toward your loved one. Without love toward your loved one, your faith and hope are entirely useless, like "a resounding gong or a clanging symbol" (1 Cor. 13:1).

As the apostle Paul suggested, since our knowledge is always limited, we must let love be our guiding light (1 Cor. 13:9–13). So, with these last four affirmations, we'll focus on ways we can demonstrate love toward our loved one in their spiritual journey, even though we may not understand—or maybe, especially because we don't understand—where they are going and why they must go that way.

LOVE AND BOUNDARIES

Love begins with a deep understanding of another person's personhood. Your loved one is a separate, unique, autonomous individual. Just as you have a sense of self and being in charge of and responsible for your own thoughts, feelings, and actions, so do they—as they should.

When two people interact with one another, the only way that interaction can be a healthy one is if both individuals have appropriate respect for the other's personhood. Having respect for the other's personhood involves paying attention to boundaries.

Personal boundaries refer to the point at which my "self" ends and another person's "self" begins. It's easy for most people to see how personal boundaries come into play in the physical world. For example, I must respect other people's autonomy over their own bodies. I have no right to walk over to a person in the produce section of the grocery store, shove them out of my way, push them to the floor, and grab the avocado they wanted. If I did that, I would be facing the possibility of assault charges.

THE RIGHT TO PERSONAL BELIEFS

What's not as easy to see, but just as important, is that personal boundaries apply to another person's thoughts and beliefs, in addition to their body. No one has the right to tell another person what to think or believe. Each person has the right to decide those things for themselves.

This brings us to the ninth affirmation:

> *I support my loved one's desire*
> *to decide what they truly believe.*

We all want our loved ones to subscribe to the truth. We also may believe that we possess the truth. What we don't always realize or acknowledge is that, despite the truth we have been given and received, we still "see through a glass, darkly" (1 Cor. 13:12; KJV). In other words, as long as we remain human and mortal, we have a limited understanding—even of the Bible.

THE BASIS FOR BELIEF

While we may be confident that we have a good understanding of the Bible and its core messages, it's important to remember that people have been reading the Bible for centuries and arriving at very different interpretations of it. In many cases, there are wide variations in how a single text is understood. There is a reason why there are literally dozens or even hundreds of commentaries in English alone on each book of the Bible. It's because none of us fully understand the Bible and even experts disagree on what it says.

What is true for Bible study is just as true—if not more so—for biblical and systematic theology. There is not only one way of understanding Christian doctrine or theology— there are many. An argument could be made that there is only one correct way to understand the Bible and theology, but how are we to decide which is true if we don't use our own brains to determine the answer for ourselves?

Many people, in fact, choose *not* to use their own brains, but to rely on the authority of people they consider wiser, more knowledgeable, or closer to God. If the preacher, professor, scholar, or theologian they trust most says it, they believe it. But this is unwise because it gives someone else—other than God—control over your thoughts and beliefs.

Rather than placing our trust in another human being, it really is up to each of us to decide for ourselves what we believe is the truth. That is your loved one's responsibility and privilege as well.

RESPECTING BOUNDARIES

By affirming that you support your loved one's desire to decide what they really believe, you're establishing a personal boundary between you and them. You are acknowledging that, while you care about your loved one very much, what they choose to believe is for them to decide—and you don't intend to take that decision away from them, nor could you if you tried.

If you refuse to establish or observe this boundary, two things are likely to happen:

> 1. You will damage your relationship with your loved one by overstepping this important boundary. They will no longer see you as a safe person.

> 2. They will continue on to decide on their own what they really believe.

In other words, not only will you drive a wedge between you and your loved one that will not be easily removed, your efforts to influence their thinking will ultimately be unsuccessful.

That means you really only have two options:

1. Respect and support your loved one's right to establish their own beliefs—and continue to have a healthy relationship with them.

2. Overstep your loved one's personal boundaries by expecting them to believe as you do—and do serious damage to your relationship with them.

Only one of these two options shows true love—the one that acknowledges your loved one's personhood and respects their personal boundaries. You don't have to agree with every decision they make or believe the way they do. But it is important that you affirm and support their right to determine for themselves what they believe.

PRACTICE AFFIRMATION 9

Here are some suggestions for practicing Affirmation 9.

THINK IT

1. Remember that this affirmation is based on all the other ones, including your new belief that your loved one's spiritual journey is leading them to spiritual maturity. Remind yourself, as often as you need to, that by allowing your loved one the space to develop their own beliefs, you are giving them permission and an opportunity to grow in their faith.

2. Spend some time thinking about the concept of personal boundaries, especially as it relates to your loved one's spiritual journey. Where do you "end" and your loved one "begin"? Determine to respect your loved one's boundaries as they continue their spiritual journey.

FEEL IT

1. Consider how you would feel if someone in your life expected you to change your beliefs to match theirs. If you refused or showed any signs of continuing to think for yourself, they would judge you and warn you that you two wouldn't be on good terms anymore. Imagine what it feels like to have your boundaries violated in that way. Using your thoughts, establish how you would feel if you violated someone else's boundaries that way.

2. After reading these instructions, close your eyes and imagine your loved one sitting here with you. Feel your respect for them as a person. Acknowledge their need to choose their own way in life. Choose to love and honor them, whatever path they find themselves on. Trust that God is guiding them to spiritual maturity.

ACT ON IT

Consider telling your loved one that you respect their need to choose what they believe and fully support them doing so. Whether you say this to them or not, let this basic respect and your understanding of personal boundaries guide how you interact with them.

AFFIRMATION 10

*I relinquish into God's hands any desire to
guide or control my loved one's journey.*

Most of us have been on the receiving end of a manipulative relationship. Manipulation involves one person seeking power over another person through their feelings. Perhaps the form of manipulation most of us are familiar with is "guilting." Guilting occurs when one person convinces another person to feel as if it would be wrong for them to do or not do what the other person wants. This is a form of emotional manipulation.

Emotional manipulation is always based on our beliefs. If someone knows what we believe, they know what would make us feel guilty and motivate us to action. Long-term manipulation can involve introducing new beliefs and later using those beliefs to elicit the feelings that will lead to the desired actions.

AWAKENING FAITH

We can see this type of manipulation clearly in the rhetoric of political parties in America. Both parties try to shape people's beliefs about the other party. I won't get into specific examples here, but think about the rhetoric you've heard against your own party. You probably consider their rhetoric to be lies that play on people's emotions to get them to vote a certain way. You can be assured that people in the other party feel the same way about your party's rhetoric.

Most adults today grew up with parents who used some form of emotional manipulation to get their children to obey. Some parents used it sparingly, only when the situation seemed to warrant it. For others, it was their default mode of "controlling" their children's behavior. One common example is when parents use their children's belief in hell to pressure them to behave in a certain way. As we learn more about manipulation and its effects, a new generation of parents is learning to raise their children in manipulation-free environments.

EMOTIONAL MANIPULATION VIOLATES PERSONHOOD

The problem with emotional manipulation is that it violates the other's personhood. As we discussed in the last chapter, people—including children—have the right to maintain control over and be responsible for their own thoughts, feelings, and actions. When someone tries to force us to feel—and then act—a certain way, they are not treating us as a person, but as an object to control, even if they seem to have very good intentions.

106

It's not always easy to see when people are manipulating us. It's even more difficult to see when we are trying to manipulate other people. That's why the tenth affirmation is so critical:

I relinquish into God's hands any desire to guide or control my loved one's journey.

I hope you can already see that this affirmation is an act of love, based on the faith and hope of the previous nine affirmations. If we believe everything we've asserted in affirmations one through nine, then it is entirely reasonable and logical to relinquish any desire for control of your loved one's spiritual journey. If you don't feel ready to make this sincere affirmation, then you may want to go back through the first nine affirmations and work to internalize them. You may have them in your head, but they haven't yet reached the stage of subconscious belief where they guide your heart.

A NEED FOR CONTROL UNDERMINES HEALTHY RELATIONSHIPS

The reason for this affirmation is simple. If you retain any desire—consciously or subconsciously—to guide or control your loved one's journey, you will find it impossible to have a healthy, meaningful, productive relationship. If you are still seeking to guide and control your loved one, you are not relating with them in love, person-to-person as equals. Instead, you are trying to relate to them from a place of superiority, as a subject to be controlled. This is not a healthy basis for a relationship.

THE WAY OF JESUS

If you need further confirmation of what I'm saying, read through the gospels. Jesus was a master over his own interactions with people—and he was certainly capable of emotional manipulation to a degree that we can only imagine. Yet, he never once went that route. He always treated people as people. He always respected personal boundaries. He loved fully and yet never forced anyone to believe or played on their guilt or fears to get them to behave in a certain way. He presented his own beliefs and vision for life, while respecting a person's right to choose their own pathway.

This is the model I'm offering you—the way of Jesus.

AVOID THE TEMPTATION TO EMOTIONAL MANIPULATION

Emotional manipulation will harm and even destroy your relationship with your loved one. Yet this is the tactic I see most often from Christians who are concerned when a loved one is exploring a different avenue in their spiritual journey.

Be on the lookout for any tendencies in yourself to manipulate your loved one emotionally. As I said, it is difficult to see and acknowledge when we are violating our loved ones' boundaries in this way. So, be overly cautious in this area. Let your loved one guide conversations about their own spiritual journey, rather than seeking to inject your point of view. Avoid any temptation to make your loved one feel any kind of way.

Even better, do the heart work required to remove this tendency from yourself. The twelve affirmations in this book are designed to help you do just that. Read them, listen to them, think on them, meditate on them, and let them sink deep into your being until they become a part of who you are—the default way in which you think and consider your relationship with your loved one. Then you will know you have placed your faith in God for this matter, rather than relying on your own plans and schemes.

PRACTICE AFFIRMATION 10

Here are some suggestions for practicing Affirmation 10.

THINK IT

1. In what ways might you harm your loved one if you were to seek to guide or control their spiritual journey based on your limited perspective and experience? How is this affirmation—to relinquish desire for control—an act of love toward your loved one?

2. Which of the earlier affirmations—or your personal beliefs—makes it easier for you to apply this one—to relinquish any desire you may feel to guide or control the outcome of your loved one's journey?

FEEL IT

Take a minute or two to imagine how it might feel if someone were trying to emotionally manipulate you in this moment. Maybe they are suggesting you will go to hell if you do something that seems relatively benign to you. Or they are subtly threatening to not be a part of your life if you continue to relate with certain people whom you know to be good people or continue talking about certain books you've read that you know to be good books. How would that make you feel? How would you respond? Would you give in to their manipulation? Would it change how you feel about them? After thinking through those questions consider how it impacts your feelings about the affirmation in this chapter.

ACT ON IT

1. If it feels appropriate and helpful to do so—and you can do it truthfully—tell your loved one that you have no desire to guide or control your journey and that you fully trust God to guide them to spiritual maturity. Then leave it at that.

2. Anytime you begin to feel anxiety about your loved one's spiritual journey, return to this affirmation. Reread the text of this chapter, and then meditate on the affirmation until you can again relinquish control to God.

11

AFFIRMATION 11

*I aim to be a positive, supportive presence
for my loved one's journey.*

Despite popular opinion, few people choose to embark on a spiritual journey like the one your loved one is pursuing. Most people who experience it feel that it has been thrust upon them, that they had no choice, that they must. They know that if they're going to continue to believe, then there are some things they have to figure out, some experiences they have to come to terms with.

Unfortunately, if your loved one is like most people who embark on such journeys, they have likely found that many of the people they were accustomed to relying on for support have now become their adversaries. Most churches are built on shared beliefs and doctrinal unity. They have little room for or tolerance of people who question those shared beliefs or explore other ways of understanding Christianity, faith, and spirituality.

It could be that your loved one's church friends have begun to withdraw from them. Their pastor or other church leaders may have already "invited them to coffee" in order to confront them about their apparent departure from the church's set of beliefs. It doesn't take long for one deconstructing their faith to learn just how fully their life has been built on a sort-of conditional agreement with the church. The message is clear: believe this and act this way, and you're one of us. Step outside the lines for very long, and we have to break up with you.

THE CHURCH'S FAILURE
TO SUPPORT
SPIRITUAL EXPLORATION

The sad reality is that, though nearly every church has something to learn from spiritual questers like your loved one, most will never benefit from those learnings, because they are so quick to exclude people who don't fully align with their beliefs and standards of behavior. They never have the benefit of learning from people with an alternative perspective.

An even sadder reality is that people like your loved one, who have chosen to be true to their conscience and wrestle with hard questions, generally experience rejection from the church. They may have invested years of their lives and a steady percentage of their income in helping the church to grow and thrive, but suddenly they may find themselves without the welcome, friendship, and support of people from that very church when they most need it.

THE GIFT OF EMPATHY

That's where you can be a great benefit to your loved one—and where affirmation eleven comes in:

I aim to be a positive, supportive presence for my loved one's journey.

A gift you can give your loved one at this important moment in their life's journey is the gift of empathy. Empathy is about temporarily putting aside your own thoughts, feelings, and point of view and seeking to enter into another person's thoughts, feelings, and point of view to see what life looks like from their perspective.

Empathy doesn't mean *adopting* the other person's perspective but *understanding* it. A good outcome from exercising empathy is to be able to say to your loved one: "I understand why you feel the way you do. While I may not feel the need to question my own faith, I understand why that's what makes most sense for you right now. And because of that, I support you in doing so."

Supporting a person who is deconstructing their faith doesn't mean that you agree with everything—or anything— they say or do. It simply means that you understand their need to do so, and you offer your supportive presence to them, rather than rejecting them or otherwise distancing yourself from them. It can also mean respecting their need to separate from the church and its influence for a time while they figure things out.

CULTIVATE POSITIVE FEELINGS

To be truly supportive, you must feel positively about your loved one. Again, you don't have to agree with their every thought or action. But you do have to believe in and have positive feelings toward the *person*.

If your loved one is like most people who deconstruct their faith, they are currently experiencing a lot of negativity from other Christians and the church. With empathy, even though you love the church, you can imagine how this makes your loved one feel. They are simply trying to work things out in their own mind and heart, and they are being maligned for seeking the truth.

YOU CAN BE A HERO

But you can be different. You can be the Christian—perhaps the only one in their life—who remains a positive, supportive presence for them. In my book, that makes you a hero.

It takes courage to support a person who is on a journey like your loved one's. You may have people criticize you for not being judgmental and critical toward them. But if you truly love your loved one, you want to give them what they need. And what they need right now is not judgment, but your positive, supportive presence in their life.

And I believe you can—and will—do it.

PRACTICE AFFIRMATION 11

Here are some suggestions for practicing Affirmation 11.

THINK IT

1. Consider the value of empathy. If we never exercised empathy, we would only ever know our own perspective and could only learn from our own experiences. What would it take for you to temporarily set aside your own perspective and enter your loved one's perspective. If you seek the truth, you truly have nothing to fear and everything to gain.

2. Think about how your loved one might perceive the church and Christianity if they are honestly seeking the truth and only receive negativity in return from other Christians. Remind yourself daily that your loved one needs your positive, supportive presence in their life.

FEEL IT

1. It's difficult to be positive and supportive if you harbor negativity in your heart toward your loved one. Examine your heart to determine whether you have any remaining negative thoughts about your loved one or their spiritual journey. If so, do the heart work to replace those negative thoughts and feelings with positive ones.

2. The Greek word *empatheia*, from which we get our English word empathy, could be literally translated as "feeling with" or "suffering with." To be a positive, sup-

portive presence for your loved one, it's helpful to learn to "feel with" them—to identify with what they're feeling, while still maintaining your own personal identity. Try to understand and even feel a bit for yourself of what your loved one is feeling.

ACT ON IT

What it looks like to be a positive, supporting presence will look differently depending on the situation. One thing that will always be helpful is to speak positively of your loved one and their journey and to help others understand the reasons for their spiritual journey.

AFFIRMATION 12

*I expect to learn and grow vicariously
through my loved one's journey.*

Christians sometimes get tripped up by thinking that they already know everything there is to know about faith, spirituality, and following the way of Jesus. We can easily forget that we—and everyone in our faith tradition from top to bottom—has a limited perspective. We all see through a glass darkly—individually and corporately.

This forgetfulness of our limited perspective is one of the main reasons that Christians almost always judge those who begin deconstructing their faith. They assume they are being unfaithful. They project that they are leaving the faith. They expect that their journey will lead to spiritual darkness.

It's worth questioning those assumptions. Just because most Christians react that way doesn't mean it's the Christian response. In fact, if every affirmation we've explored in this book is true—I think they are, and presumably since you've made it this far, you do too—then there is a good reason to hope and expect that your loved one will learn something on their spiritual journey that could benefit other Christians and the entire church. We all see through a glass darkly, but it's reasonable to think that a diligent seeker of the truth can add at least a tiny bit of clarity to the overall picture. If we reject that possibility, we've made an idol of our own doctrine or point of view, which is far worse than being open to truths we've not yet learned or experienced.

That brings us to the twelfth and final affirmation:

*I expect to learn and grow vicariously
through my loved one's journey.*

What I want you to see is that this is the truly faithful response to your loved one's spiritual journey. In your loved one's journey to ascertain the truth, they are not likely to uncover the whole truth, but if they are diligent, they are almost guaranteed to uncover some part of the truth that you and others around you have overlooked or ignored.

If you assume that your loved one is undertaking their journey—as I believe—out of faithfulness to the truth more than unfaithfulness to God or the church, it changes everything. If you are willing to consider that the church as a whole sees through a glass darkly, then it becomes clear that questioning the church's doctrines is not necessarily unfaithfulness to God.

One can be both a seeker of the truth and a critic of the church—and that may be precisely where your loved one is at this point. To disregard out of hand the possibility that your loved one may be on to something may represent greater unfaithfulness to God than their journey does. The established church certainly didn't accept and endorse Martin Luther's deconstruction of accepted doctrine—or any number of the other reformers, many of whom contributed to our spiritual understanding.

The point is, if we are unable or unwilling to consider where the church may be wrong—even historically wrong—then we have already made the church and its doctrine an idol. This affirmation is a strong counterpoint that makes it clear that we do not make the church or its doctrine infallible. Christians believe in a church and a set of doctrines that can—and should—be continually reforming, as believers seek and receive more of the truth.

So, I encourage you to consider and embrace as much as you can the truth that your loved one may have something to teach you, that their journey gives you an opportunity to grow. You may not adopt their point of view as a whole—or you might. But I am confident there will be something that you can learn, embrace, and allow to refresh your perspective and point of view. Your loved one can help awaken your faith to a higher level than you've experienced before.

In many ways, this is the most challenging and "advanced" of the affirmations. That's why it sits here at the end of the list. If you struggle with this one, your relationship with your loved one will still benefit greatly from internalizing the other eleven. But this is where you have the opportunity to experience the most growth in your own life.

And I trust that you will find your way to doing so—if not now, then at some point in the future. Things will click, and you'll understand that no one individual or institution has the corner on spiritual truth. And you'll be grateful to your loved one for having the courage to launch out on this spiritual journey that has taught you so much.

WRAPPING UP THE FOUR AFFIRMATIONS OF LOVE

Now we've completed the four affirmations of love. Let's recap:

9. I support my loved one's desire to decide what they truly believe.

10. I relinquish into God's hands any desire to guide or control my loved one's journey.

11. I aim to be a positive, supportive presence for my loved one's journey.

12. I expect to learn and grow vicariously through my loved one's journey.

Sometimes our beliefs—even beliefs we consider Christian—cause us to act in a way that introduces brokenness into a relationship. This happens when we seek to pressure, manipulate, or control our loved one and help them "see the truth."

The loving response is to respect our loved one's boundaries, support them in their journey, and love them for who they are rather than who we might wish they would be, all while trusting God to bring about the results he desires in their life. These four statements affirm your desire to show genuine love throughout your loved one's spiritual journey, wherever it might lead.

PRACTICE AFFIRMATION 12

Here are some suggestions for practicing Affirmation 12.

THINK IT

1. Read through all twelve affirmations together. To make this easier, the appendix contains the full list, in order. As you read, note which affirmations still give you internal reservations. Those internal reservations are an indication that you haven't fully allowed those beliefs to reach the subconscious level. Continue to work specifically on those beliefs by focusing additional attention on those affirmations in coming weeks.

2. If you haven't already done so, find a way to bring these affirmations to mind regularly. Post them in a location in your home where you will see and read them frequently. Write them in a note on your phone, and set a reminder to review them every morning and evening. Sign up for my weekly email at kevinrscott.com for additional support and reinforcement.

FEEL IT

1. Read through all 12 affirmations again. Note which affirmations give you a positive emotional response. You feel that they are true, more than just knowing it. This is the level of affirmation that you are seeking for all 12 affirmations.

2. If there are affirmations that still do not feel true, even though you are trying to believe them, spend some time

exploring what beliefs you currently hold that might be in contradiction to those beliefs. Then seek to adapt those contradicting beliefs so that they support your affirmation.

ACT ON IT

Over time, internalizing these affirmations will transform your relationship with your loved one. Take a moment to thank God, in advance, for helping you to become a positive, supportive presence in your loved one's life, and ask God for wisdom in seeking to learn from your loved one's journey.

If you have stories to share about how these affirmations have benefited you and enhanced your relationship with your loved one, I would love to hear them. You can send your story to admin@kevinrscott.com.

APPENDIX
THE TWELVE AFFIRMATIONS

AFFIRMATIONS OF FAITH

1. God's love for my loved one is infinite.
2. God is with my loved one on their journey.
3. God is at work in my loved one's life in ways beyond my understanding.
4. God is pleased by my loved one's search for truth.

AFFIRMATIONS OF HOPE

5. My loved one's heart is in the right place.
6. My loved one is smart enough to figure things out.
7. My loved one is on the right path for them (even if I can't see it right now).
8. My loved one's journey is leading to greater spiritual maturity.

AFFIRMATIONS OF LOVE

9. I support my loved one's desire to decide what they truly believe.
10. I relinquish into God's hands any desire to guide or control my loved one's journey.
11. I aim to be a positive, supportive presence for my loved one's journey.
12. I expect to learn and grow vicariously through my loved one's journey.

DID YOU BENEFIT FROM THIS BOOK?

I'd love to hear your story!
Send me a message at admin@kevinrscott.com.

ALSO CONSIDER . . .

- Giving a copy of the book to others who could benefit from reading it.
- Following me on social media.
- Reading my first book, *ReCreatable: How God Heals the Brokenness of Life*.
- Visiting my online space at kevinrscott.com.

www.ingramcontent.com/pod-product-compliance
Lightning Source LLC
Chambersburg PA
CBHW022100020426
42335CB00012B/768